Set an Example

TIM CHALLIES

CRUCIFORM PRESS | DECEMBER 2017

CruciformPress
ⓒ CHALLIES

AUTHOR

Tim Challies is a Christian, a husband to Aileen, and a father to three children aged 11 to 17. He is a co-founder of Cruciform Press and has written several books, including *Visual Theology*, *Do More Better*, and *Sexual Detox*. He worships and serves as a pastor at Grace Fellowship Church in Toronto, Ontario and writes daily at www.challies.com.

 *We all know the feeling: every week, every month, every year it just seems that life keeps moving faster and faster. So we've taken our trademark length—books of about 100 pages—and added a set of resources that will make for even a quicker read. Cruciform Quick: a new line of booklets in the range of 40 to 60 pages each.*

SET AN EXAMPLE

Print / PDF ISBN: 978-1-941114-33-9
Mobipocket ISBN: 978-1-941114-34-6
ePub ISBN: 978-1-941114-35-3

Table of Contents

The Calling of an Artist

I was always lousy at painting. Hopeless, even. In my high-school art classes the teacher would give the kind of assignment that involved studying a car or a human form or a bowl of fruit. Our task was to observe and then paint. I would do what she said. I would look at the subject, I would study it, I would observe its form, its curves, its angles, its colors, its shadows. But when I put brush to paper, the result would never look like it was supposed to. It didn't look realistic, and it didn't look impressionistic or abstract. It just looked like a mess. It's for good reason that I skipped fine arts in college so I could pursue liberal arts—English, history, humanities. That was where I was meant to be.

Yet there is still an area where I know I have the calling of the artist. I may not have the eye, the hand, the skill for painting, but I believe God has given me everything I need to succeed at this other form of art. Francis Schaeffer describes it like this: "No work of art is more important than the Christian's own life, and every Christian is called upon to be an artist in this sense.... The Christian's life is to be a thing of truth and also a thing of beauty in the midst of a lost and despairing world." That's a work of art I want to create. That's a work of art God calls and equips each one of us to create. Even you.

I have prepared this little booklet with younger Christians in mind. If you are sixteen or eighteen or in your twenties, if you are in high school or college or just moving into marriage and career, I want to speak to you. I want to speak *with* you. I hope you will listen to what I say and hear me out. Best of all, I hope you'll read the Scripture passages I refer to, that you will pray about them and ask God to help you apply them to your life. After all, those words are God's words, meant to lead you to God's will.

As we go, I want to focus on one key verse. It will be our theme and we will return to it again and again. "Let no one despise you for your youth, but set the believers an example in speech, in conduct, in love, in faith, in purity" (1 Timothy 4:12). In these words we encounter art, we encounter the ideas of modeling and imitation, of studying a form and attempting to recreate it. But this art does not exist on paper or on canvas. This art exists in a life. A Christian life. Your life is the canvas.

Before I close out this introduction, we ought to back up just a few verses. In verse 7 of the same chapter Paul employs a different metaphor. He walks down the hall from the art room to the weight room. "Train yourself for godliness; for while bodily training is of some value, godliness is of value in every way, as it holds promise for the present life and also for the life to come" (1 Timothy 4:7b–8). Physical training is good, whether you're training for strength, speed, agility, or distance. But this kind of physical training needs to take a back seat to spiritual training—training in godliness. Shaping your character is so much more important than shaping your body. The kind of formation that concerns God most is not physical but spiritual. Both are good, but one is better.

There are many good ways to invest your time at this stage of life, but none is better than the pursuit of godliness. As we saw in our key verse, the Bible calls you to be an example in speech, conduct, love, faith, and purity. We will see that these five terms speak to your inner and outer self, to what you think and what you say, to what is hidden in your heart and what is broadcast in your life. We will see that God means for your life to be a canvas, the setting for a beautiful work of art. And he also expects this work of art will be seen, admired, and imitated.

I hope you'll stick with me as we learn how you can train yourself to be an example to others, even to people far older than you.

CHAPTER 1

Set an Example

As you know, our key verse is 1 Timothy 4:12: "Let no one despise you for your youth, but set the believers an example in speech, in conduct, in love, in faith, in purity." What we want to do is begin to dig into those five words, those five ways in which Paul challenges Timothy to be exemplary. But before we can get to them, we have a number of other matters to sort out. What does Paul mean when he refers to Timothy as a youth? Why does Timothy need to be concerned with being despised? And what does it even mean for Timothy to set an example? Only after we have answered these questions will we be ready to discuss the character traits Timothy needs to exemplify: speech, conduct, love, faith, and purity.

THE MATTER OF YOUTH

We need to back up just a little to set the context of our passage. We are reading a 2,000-year-old letter written by the Apostle Paul to Pastor Timothy. Paul is the older man, the mentor, while Timothy is the younger man, the disciple. Paul has traveled with Timothy, taught with him, suffered with him, planted and pastored with him. They've been together so long and through so much that later on Paul can remind him, "you have followed my teaching, my conduct, my aim in life, my faith, my patience, my love, my steadfastness, my persecutions and sufferings" (2 Timothy 3:10-11). Paul has modeled Christian living and Timothy has imitated him. Now Timothy is settling in as pastor to the church in Ephesus while Paul has moved on to take the gospel even farther, to plant even more churches.

But Paul is a good mentor, a good friend. Though he has moved on, he has not forgotten Timothy. He knows his strengths and weaknesses, his struggles and temptations. He also knows all about his calling as a pastor, a church leader. All of that comes into his mind as he sits down to write this letter of encouragement, of guidance and instruction. As we come to our verse we hear Paul tell Timothy, "Let no one despise you for your youth." That's a command, an order. "Don't allow it! Don't allow anyone in that church to despise you for your youth."

We read the word "youth" today and picture Timothy as a guy in his late teens or early twenties, a person in the youth group or maybe just starting in to college and careers. But as we read about the life of Paul and do a little basic math, we realize that Timothy was quite a bit older than that—probably closer to his mid-thirties. That is all grown up in our reckoning, but in that culture he may as well have been a fresh-faced young man just clutching his college degree. In Timothy's day, forty was considered the age of maturity and those who were older were not inclined to think well of anyone who was younger. They certainly were not likely to think that younger people could be a worthwhile example to follow. Even Christians would be tempted to believe that maturity of character demanded at least forty years of age. In that day, in that city, Timothy was young.

DON'T SURRENDER TO LOW EXPECTATIONS

But still Paul tells him, "Let no one despise you for your youth." If the word "despise" seems a bit strong, then maybe we can offer some alternatives like "look down on," or "hold in contempt." Now you see it, right? Paul doesn't want Timothy to give people reason to look down on him because he is young. He doesn't want Timothy to lack confidence that even at his age he can serve as a model of Christian maturity. He doesn't want Timothy to surrender to their low expectations, to do sinful things and give them cause to say, "I knew it! I knew he would do that because he's so young!"

Have you ever felt something like that? Have you felt the weight, the pain of these low expectations? Have you encountered older people who act like there is nothing they could learn from you, not when you're only sixteen or eighteen or twenty-two? Have you felt like you have nothing to contribute, like anything you say will just generate awkward silences or rolling eyes? Have you become convinced that older people are looking down on you for no better reason than that you are young? You probably have at one time or another. So keep reading. Keep reading because what Paul says next is beautiful and counter-cultural. He doesn't tell Timothy to demand the respect of those older Christians. He doesn't allow Timothy to feel sorry for himself or to plead with those older people to respect him. No, Paul has a far better solution.

HOW TO SET AN EXAMPLE

"Let no one despise you for your youth, but set the believers an example..." How is Timothy to head off the older people's tendency toward disrespect? How is he to avoid getting into a position where he has messed up and everyone is now looking at him with that "I told you so" look in their eye? By setting an example. By serving as a model of godliness. He is to be the kind of person that older Christians will have to respect because they will see his humble, godly character and his pure, selfless conduct.

Timothy is to "set an example." This is a term related to art. When you are in art class, the teacher may put a model in the middle of the room and tell you to paint it or sculpt it. That is the example and you, the artist, are to study it, to learn everything about it, and then to make your best reproduction. In this case, the work of art is Timothy's life. He is to live a life of public godliness and to be such an example that others will see this work of art and imitate it. Even older people who are inclined to disrespect him will see his life and understand that he is modeling Christian thought and Christian living. They will be drawn to his example as he far exceeds their low expectations.

Timothy isn't to worry about what other people think of him. He isn't to demand respect by force of will or force of personality. He is to earn respect by the way he lives. John Stott says, "People would not despise his youth if they could admire his example." And this is true of you, too. The people around you, old or young, will not be distracted by your youth if they can admire your example. And you, like Timothy, actually can be an example. In fact, God calls you to be an example. Your youth is no excuse for ungodliness or spiritual immaturity. Right now, today, God calls you to set an example —an example of godliness, of character, of maturity.

There are many ways you can serve your church. You can care for the children in the nursery, you can stack the chairs in the back of the room, you can direct cars in the parking lot. These are all good things, all good ways of serving others. Keep doing these things and keep looking for opportunities to serve. But the biggest way, the best way, the primary way to serve your church is to pursue godliness, to grow in wisdom and knowledge, in character and obedience. Set an example. Be an example. Make your life a beautiful work of art.

In our next chapter we will begin to look at the traits Timothy is to exemplify: speech, conduct, love, faith, and purity. We will begin, of course, with speech: "Set the believers an example in your speech. But first, here are some questions you may wish to consider as you begin to apply the truths we have learned."

QUESTIONS TO CONSIDER

1. *Can you think of times when you felt older Christians were looking down on you because of your age? Did they have good reason to? How did you respond?*

2. *Read Philippians 2:1-11 and consider what Jesus models there. Did he demand respect or was he content to set an example? In what ways did Jesus serve the church?*

3. *Paul invested so much time in Timothy that Timothy began to imitate Paul in his thought and behavior. Is there someone in your life you'd like to mentor you in that way? What can you do about it? Is there someone in your life who may be wishing that you would offer to mentor them? What can you do about it?*

4. *In what ways do you think you are setting a good example to the people of your church? Pray and thank God for each of them. In what ways do you think you are not setting a good example to the people of your church? Pray and ask God for his grace to change you.*

CHAPTER 2

Set an Example
in Your Speech

Last summer I spent one beautiful day in Cambridge, England. I was there to participate in a writing workshop and that day we were given one afternoon to ourselves to do whatever we wished. Since I was not feeling particularly creative in that moment, I decided to explore the town. I happened across a museum and, since it was free, thought I'd take a look. I wandered through exhibit after exhibit, admiring ancient and medieval antiquities—pottery, sculptures, mummies, weapons, and on and on. My time was nearly up when I came to one final room that held a collection of paintings. I was shocked to suddenly find myself among the masters. There on the wall were paintings by Rubens, Monet, Matisse, and many more. I had no idea this little museum had amassed such an impressive collection. There was something inspiring about being in the presence of greatness, inches from the works of history's most renowned artists.

We respond with awe and respect when we are in the presence of those who are at the top of their field. We admire them and want to be like them. This is why we are investing effort in this extended study of 1 Timothy 4:12. To this point we've taken a look at the first part of our text: "Let no one despise you for your youth, but set the believers an example..." We saw Paul the mentor telling young Timothy not to give in to the low expectations of the people around him. Timothy needed to understand that even as a younger person he was meant to make his life a work of art that others could see, admire, and imitate.

Now we begin to look at the specific ways Timothy is to set an example, to be that work of art. "Let no one despise you for your youth, but set the believers an example in speech, in conduct, in love, in faith, in purity."

There are 5 areas in which Timothy is to serve as an example to other believers:

- in his speech
- in his conduct
- in his love
- in his faith
- in his purity

These traits fall into two groupings. Speech and conduct are primarily displayed outwardly while love, faith, and purity are primarily traits of the inner self. Thus Timothy is to ensure that his words and deeds are admirable and also to examine his heart to ensure his love, faith, and purity are equally exemplary. He has to understand that these inner traits will eventually display themselves through what he says and does. We are going to examine these traits one by one and make them applicable to you and to me. Our first challenge is to consider what it means to set an example in your speech.

THE POWER OF WORDS

You do not need to read far into the Bible to see the power of words. Actually, you only need to get to the third verse of the first book to see it. In Genesis 1:3 God speaks and begins to bring the world into existence. By the end of chapter 2 he has spoken into being everything that is, including humanity. He has declared that everything he has made is good and very good. God's words are powerful!

Then chapter 3 comes and we begin to see the danger of

misusing words. There is a lot of speaking here. Satan speaks words meant to deceive human beings, Adam speaks words meant to blame his wife for his own sin, Eve speaks words meant to deflect the blame from herself. By the time all is said and done, the world will never be the same. We turn to Genesis 4 and find that brothers are killing brothers and lying to God about it, Lamech is making outrageous boasts about his own importance, and it only gets worse from there. Words can cause so much good. Words can cause so much harm.

It is no surprise, then, that the Bible addresses our words. It is no surprise that Paul addresses Timothy's words: "Set the believers an example in speech." As Paul says this, he uses one of those Greek words you may already know: *logos*. It's the word for *word*, for the communication that comes out of our mouths—or, by extension, the words that come out through our thumbs or fingers when we type and tap rather than speak.

OUT OF THE OVERFLOW

Paul wants young pastor Timothy to know that his words have the power to make or break his ministry. His words can help others or harm them, they can encourage others or destroy them. As a preacher and leader Timothy will be speaking a lot of words, and every one of them will have the power to prove him an example to follow or a disaster to avoid.

Why are words so important? Jesus gives the answer in Luke 6:45: "Out of the abundance of the heart the mouth speaks." The alarming truth is that the mouth reveals what is in the heart. It is like the heart overflows so that what is in the heart comes pouring out of the mouth. Ugly words reveal an inner ugliness and beautiful words reveal an inner beauty. James asks "Does a spring pour forth from the same opening both fresh and salt water" (James 3:11)? Obviously not. Salty water comes from a salty spring just like salty words come from a salty heart.

Paul knew all of this and wanted Timothy to know it as well. In his other letters Paul insists that some ways of speaking are completely inappropriate for Christians and must be avoided at all costs. These are the kinds of speech associated with the old man, the old way of living: falsehood, anger, bitterness, slander, malice, abusive speech, and filthy talk. All of these are unsuitable for Christians and will damage their credibility. Other, better ways of speaking are to be pursued, and these are the ones associated with the new man, the new way of living: truth, edification, admonition, tenderness, forgiveness, and thanks. These are suitable for Christians and give evidence of their holiness and spiritual maturity.[1]

Timothy's challenge was to put to death all those old ways of speaking and to bring to life all those new ways of speaking. He was to ensure that every word that came out of his mouth was good, true, and exemplary. His ministry, his credibility, his usefulness to God depended on it.

Timothy's challenge is your challenge. Today's world gives you more opportunities than ever to use your words— to express them face to face, of course, but also to type them into Facebook, to tap them into a text message, to speak them through Snapchat. You communicate constantly and every one of your words matters. Every one of your words displays your heart. Do your words set an example for others to imitate?

QUESTIONS TO CONSIDER

1. *Who have you known who has set an example of the kind of speech the Bible commends?*

2. *The biblical pattern for overcoming sin is always "put off" and then "put on," or it's "put to death" old patterns and habits and then "bring to life" new patterns and habits. When it comes to your speech, what are some sinful ways of speaking that you need to put off or put to death? What are some virtuous ways of speaking that you need to put on or bring to life?*

3. *Consider how some of these proverbs should challenge you. "When words are many, transgression is not lacking" (10:19). "Whoever guards his mouth preserves his life" (13:3). "The heart of the righteous ponders how to answer, but the mouth of the wicked pours out evil things" (15:28). "If one gives an answer before he hears, it is his folly and shame" (18:13). Why don't you ask another person to evaluate you in light of these proverbs?*

4. *In what ways do you think you are setting a good example to the people of your church in the way you speak? Pray and thank God for each of them. In what ways do you think you are not setting a good example to the people of your church in the way you speak? Pray and ask God for his grace to change you.*

CHAPTER 3

Set an Example
in Your Conduct

I want to scare you a little. At the very least I want to intimidate you. Actually, I want the Bible to scare and intimidate you, to set a challenge so difficult that you'll know you can't possibly meet it on your own.

By now you know the words that Paul, the older mentor, wrote to Timothy, his younger protégé: "Let no one despise you for your youth, but set the believers an example in speech, in conduct, in love, in faith, in purity" (1 Timothy 4:12). We've already seen that Paul wants Timothy to make his life a work of art that other people will be able to see and imitate. Even as a young man, Timothy is to be exemplary, to be worthy of imitation. We have already seen what it means for Timothy to set an example in his speech and, by extension, what it means for you to set an example in your speech. Now we need to see what it means to set an example in conduct.

THE POWER OF EXAMPLE

I'm sure you know that, as a Christian, you are meant to live as an example in the way you behave. Older siblings are warned to be a good example to their younger brothers and sisters. Christian young people are told of the importance of living as Christians before a watching world of unbelievers. When you're at school and work, when you're interacting with neighbors and customers, even when you're at a family reunion, you are to behave in distinctly Christian ways. You won't do what unbelievers do, you won't watch what unbelievers watch, you won't laugh at the things unbelievers laugh at. You are to live as salt and light, standing out from the world around you (Matthew 5:13-16). You know that. You've been told.

But did you know that you are also to stand as an example of Christian character and maturity before other Christians, even when those Christians are older, wiser, and godlier than you? That is a scary thought, an intimidating challenge. Yet this was exactly Paul's challenge to Timothy. Timothy was a young man, young enough that older Christians might look down on him, convinced that they couldn't possibly learn anything from somebody so much younger. And still Paul told him that it was his responsibility to set them an example in his conduct.

Conduct is a general word. It's a broad word that refers to all of life. In all he does, in all his behavior, Timothy is to set an example. In every realm of life he is to be exemplary. There is no area of life that isn't covered by "set the believers an example in conduct." This was true for Timothy and it is true of you. You aren't exempted from serving as an example of Christian conduct simply because you are young. You are to be an example "at home, at church, at the grocery store, on the freeway, on the playground, at the barber shop."[2] Bryan Chapell says, "In the day-in, day-out humdrum of existence—at the gas station, in the grocery line, at the soccer game, washing the car—[you] must be an example to all who believe."[3] All the time, in every way, in all of life, God challenges you to be an example of godliness to other Christians.

Are you that example of godliness? Do other believers look to you as someone who models what it means to conduct yourself as a Christian? I will leave it to you to consider the entirety of your life because I want to focus on just one area—the way you behave when you're with your local church. When you gather with other Christians, do they see you modeling Christian conduct? Do other Christians, even older Christians, see you as a model of godliness? This is your God-given task!

From the perspective of an older Christian, one who has recently entered into my forties, I can attest that few things are more encouraging to me than being around young people who exemplify Christian character. I love to be challenged by seeing young people lead godly lives. Believe it or not, their godliness is a tremendous blessing and challenge to me and to others like me. I want to challenge you to make a point of setting the believers an example in your conduct right there in your church family. Let me offer just a few ways young Christians can do this.

Be there. Attend every service. Make church attendance a high priority that will only be interrupted in the most unusual circumstances. If a sport or other activity is going to keep you from church week after week, you need to think long and hard about whether that's a fair trade. Don't let every cough and sniffle keep you home on a Sunday morning. Get your homework done by Saturday so you can commit Sunday to the Lord. Ask your boss if you can have Sundays off. You can only be an example to other people if you are around other people.

Be all-in. Once you get to church, be all-in. One of the best ways to do this is to be friendly, to meet people and engage them in conversation. Your temptation will be to gravitate to the people who are most similar to you, so challenge yourself to meet people who are different from you—much older or younger, a different ethnicity, people with disabilities. Look for people who are otherwise overlooked and get to know them. Speaking once more as someone older than you, I can testify that it is a great blessing to be greeted by younger Christians and to have them engage me in conversation.

Be a servant. Look for ways to serve in the church, and especially in those ministries that are low-visibility. Lots of people feel specially called and equipped to sing or play an instrument at the front of the room, but most of us are far better equipped to take out the trash or set up the chairs. Volunteer for the lowest jobs, the ones no one else wants to do. And then do those jobs with joy and without demanding gratitude. Be content to be overlooked.

Be visible. Yet even as you are willing to be invisible, don't be afraid to be visible. As you worship, set the believers an example in your joyful singing. As you listen to sermons, set the believers an example in your attentive listening. As you put what you've learned into practice, set the believers an example in your humility and diligence. As you fellowship, set the believers an example in your willingness to go outside your comfort zone. Remember, the very idea behind being an example is to be seen—to be seen so you can be imitated.

This is only a start, just a few suggestions. In these ways and many more you can set an example to the believers in your conduct. This is God's high and holy calling for you, the young Christian. Will you heed that call?

QUESTIONS TO CONSIDER

1. *Does it intimidate you to know that you're called by God to serve as an example in your conduct, even (and especially!) before other Christians? Why?*

2. *In what ways do you think you are serving as a good example in your conduct? Pray and thank God for them. In what ways do you think you are setting a*

poor example in your conduct? Pray and ask God to forgive you and to give you the grace to change.

3. What are some of the ways you serve in your local church? What are some of the ways you think you ought to serve in your local church?

4. Do you find it difficult or unnatural to fellowship with people who are different from you? Why do you think that is? What will you do about it?

CHAPTER 4

Set an Example
in Your Love

Art comes in many different forms. Visit a museum or art gallery and you may see sculpture, pottery, calligraphy, and, of course, paintings. Though each of these is beautiful and valuable in its own way, the Bible commends a very different form of art, one that is more important and more enduring. It is a living art, the unique artwork of the Christian. As Francis Schaeffer said, "No work of art is more important than the Christian's own life, and every Christian is called upon to be an artist in this sense." No work of art is more beautiful, more precious, than a life lived for God in imitation of his Son.

In 1 Timothy 4, Paul writes to Timothy to tell him that he is responsible for making his life just such a work of art. He is to "set an example" before other Christians, and especially the ones in his local church. Though he is still young, he is to have confidence in his ability to live an exemplary life. Now that we have looked at what it means for Timothy to set an example in his speech and conduct, we are prepared to consider his love. And through Timothy, of course, we will consider your love.

THE CHIEF OF ALL GRACES

"Let no one despise you for your youth," said Paul, "but set the believers an example in speech, in conduct, in love…" We have already seen that speech and conduct refer to the two ways Timothy's behavior would manifest itself externally—

through his words and through his actions. Timothy was to ensure that everything he said and everything he did was worthy of imitation. Paul now begins to challenge Timothy in his inner qualities. Even in the inner man he is to be exemplary, to serve as a model of Christian virtue and maturity.

It is no surprise that love heads up Paul's list of inner virtues, for love is the chief of all graces. As he says elsewhere, "Now faith, hope, and love abide, these three; but the greatest of these is love" (1 Corinthians 13:13). Love is a defining trait for a Christian: "Let us love one another, for love is from God, and whoever loves has been born of God and knows God. Anyone who does not love does not know God because God is love" (1 John 4: 7- 8). Love is to mark everything we do: "Let all that you do be done in love" (1 Co 16:14). But what is love? What is the love Timothy was meant to have?

If you have been around churches for any length of time, you have probably encountered the Greek word Paul uses here: *agape* (a-GOP-ay). You probably also know that Greek has several different words that we translate as "love," each with its own nuances. *Agape* is as straightforward as they come. It refers to esteem or affection, regard or concern. Timothy was to search his heart to ensure he was concerned for the people in his church, that he desired what was best for them, that he was eager to equip and protect them, and even that he felt affection for them. His heart was to be warm, not cool toward the people in his church. All the while he was to know that what he felt and believed internally would eventually manifest itself externally.

MORE THAN A FEELING

We need to understand that according to the Bible, love is not just feeling or emotion but something that works itself out in action. Love is not less than what we feel, but it is certainly more. Aren't you glad that Jesus did not only *feel* love for you but that he ultimately *acted* in love for you? His feelings alone would not have done you much good! In the same way, the ultimate measure of your love is not what you feel for others but what you do for them. Paul's concern was not just that Timothy feel love for others, but that he act in loving ways.

Why was this something Paul needed to mention specifically? Because people are hard to love! Loving others is the kind of challenge that tests the best of men. It is a challenge because of sin—we are sinful and they are sinful, and there is always trouble when sin meets sin. Yet loving the hard-to-love is how we demonstrate our obedience to God. It is how we demonstrate our conformity to him since, after all, Christ loved us even though we were so hard to love. It is how we display Christ-like humility. Ultimately, it is how we give evidence of our salvation. The love we extend to others is the very same love God has extended to us through Christ.

AN EXEMPLARY LOVE

Young Timothy was to be an example of Christian love, love he felt internally and love he acted on externally. The special setting for his love was his local church, for it was there that he was to set an example before other believers. Timothy's challenge is your challenge. You, too, are called to love. You are called to love the people in your local church and to serve as a model of what it means to love them well, to love them creatively, to love them thoroughly, to love them even—especially!—if they are hard to love. They may be hard to love because they are difficult people. They may be hard to love because they are so different from you—older, younger, in a different stage of life, educated a different way, a different ethnicity. They may be hard to love because you are shy and they are bold. But the challenge remains.

Each of us has a comfort zone. Each of us has a group of people who make us comfortable and other groups that make us uncomfortable. Within the church, our love needs to extend beyond any comfort zone. Your love needs to extend beyond your comfort zone. The church is to be a community of people who love one another despite differences, who love one another through differences, who love one another because of differences. It is the place where God showcases what he is doing in this world by calling all kinds of people to himself and binding them together in a spiritual family. Your church needs you to be an example of a Christian marked by love, a Christian who displays inner transformation by outward actions. Your church needs you to serve Christ by serving his people, the people he bought with his blood.

Let me offer you a challenge. Try to begin a friendship—a real friendship—with someone in your church who is at least 10 years older than you. Try to begin a friendship with someone who is at least 10 years younger than you. Try to begin a friendship with someone who is disabled. You don't need to do all of this today or this week, but over the coming weeks and months, see if you can form genuine friendships with people who are different from you. You will benefit, they will benefit, and God will receive the glory.

QUESTIONS TO CONSIDER

1. *Who do you know who sets the believers an example in his or her love? How does that person display love for others? What do you see in his or her life that you can imitate?*

2. *Consider what A.W. Pink says: "The measure of our love for others can largely be determined by the frequency and earnestness of our prayers for them." Do you pray for others? How can you pray for them with greater frequency and earnestness?*

3. *Who in your church is overlooked or unloved? Is there something you can do about it?*

4. *In what ways do you think you are setting a good example to the people of your church in the way you love others? Pray and thank God for each of them. In what ways do you think you are not setting a good example to the people of your church in the way you love others? Pray and ask God for his grace to change you.*

CHAPTER 5

Set an Example *in Your Faith*

Children are mimics. Children are mimics because human beings learn by imitation. We learn to speak by hearing our parents speak. We learn to do dishes by watching mom and dad do dishes. We even learn to love (or not love) Jesus by seeing our parents love (or not love) Jesus. In both vice and virtue, children will begin to look like their parents. Parents quickly come to realize the importance of setting a good example, of being worthy of imitation.

When Paul wrote instructions to young pastor Timothy, he told him to serve as an example to his church. "Let no one despise you for your youth, but set the believers an example in speech, in conduct, in love, in faith, in purity" (1 Timothy 4:12). Timothy was to model godly thinking and living, and to know that his church would inevitably imitate him. For good or for ill, they would begin to resemble their pastor. I have been doing my best to challenge you to heed this same call, to set the believers an example. Though you are young, though people may look down on you for your youth, still you are responsible before God and your Christian brothers and sisters to serve as an example.

Now the time has come to consider what it means to have an exemplary faith, the kind of faith that, if imitated by others, will lead them to become more like Christ. Do you have that kind of faith? If people imitate you, will they in fact be imitating Jesus? This is no small challenge!

A FAITHFUL FAITH

Though we are considering faith, we must be careful not to sever faith from love, the word it follows. In Paul's letters he often bundles the two words together. He does this twice in Thessalonians, three times in his letters to Timothy, and once in his letter to Philemon. Here are a couple of examples: "But now that Timothy has come to us from you, and has brought us the good news of your faith and love..." And, "I thank my God always when I remember you in my prayers, because I hear of your love and of the faith that you have..." We aren't positive why Paul so often links these words, but I suppose it is that both are necessary marks of a Christian. A Christian must have faith and display faith. A Christian must have love and display love. A Christian without faith and love is no Christian at all. When we see Paul tell Timothy to set the believers an example in love, it comes as no surprise that he immediately mentions faith as well.

When we consider what Paul means by faith, we are faced with two options. It could be that Paul is telling Timothy he needs to set an example in his faith: his confidence in God, his trust in God, his reliance on God for salvation and all that follows it. These are internal things. On the other hand, it could be that Paul is telling Timothy he needs to set an example in his faith*fulness*: in his *living out* of that saving faith, his commitment to the Christian life, his fidelity to all the Bible commands of him as a Christian and as a minister. The original Greek can support both options, and commentaries by expert theologians are roughly divided between the two. John Stott says the Greek word, "could mean either trust in God and in Christ, or trustworthiness, a fundamental Christian fidelity, or both."[4] But I wonder whether we actually need to pick between them since they are so closely related. You must have faith to be faithful and cannot have true faith without displaying faithfulness. The deepest faith leads to the most faithful Christian living.

So perhaps it's best to conclude that Paul primarily wants Timothy to set an example in his faith, in his unshakeable confidence in Jesus Christ, in his trust in the Word of God, in his reliance on the promises of God, and in all Paul had taught him as his friend and pastor and mentor. Charles Spurgeon says: "Faith is believing that Christ is what He is said to be, and that He will do what He has promised to do, and then to expect this of Him."[5] Paul certainly wanted no less than that for his young friend. He wanted Timothy to have an exemplary faith. If a person in his church were to ask, "What does it mean to *have faith*?" they should be able to look at Timothy to find their answer.

THE FAITHFUL CHRISTIAN

Paul knew that the person who has that kind of wholehearted reliance on God will necessarily live a steadfast life. His faith will lead to faithfulness. Jerry Bridges says, "The faithful person is one who is dependable, trustworthy, and loyal, who can be depended upon in all of his relationships, and who is absolutely honest and ethical in all of his affairs."[6] His rock-solid assurance in God is not confined to his inner man, but comes flowing out in all of life and in every one of life's decisions and responsibilities. His faith is too good, too strong, to remain hidden. Timothy is to display this exemplary faithfulness, to have a full-out commitment to living out every word of Scripture. He is to commit himself to obedience, to holiness, to love. If a person in his church were to ask, "What does it mean to *be faithful*?" they should be able to look at Timothy to find their answer.

Paul wanted Timothy to know that as he lived, served, and ministered before his church, he was to be an example of faith *and* faithfulness. He was to have that strong inner faith as well as evidence of the outward working of that faith. Though he was younger than so many members of his church, still he was to see this as his responsibility. He was to be confident that, even as a younger man, he actually could have a faith and faithfulness worthy of imitation.

Timothy's faith would begin with Scripture, with an unshakeable confidence in the truth and truthfulness of the Bible. The very next words Paul writes to Timothy is, "Devote yourself to the public reading of Scripture, to exhortation, to teaching.... Practice these things, immerse yourself in them, so that all may see your progress." Timothy was to fill himself with the Word, then to let that Word flow back out of him. His faith in the Word and the God of the Word would overflow into faithfulness.

And this is your challenge as a young person in the church today. You are to have faith, faith that is rooted and grounded in God as he reveals himself through the Word. Fill yourself with the Word. Be a man or woman of the Word. Devote yourself to Scripture. As you do this, your faith will grow, and as your faith grows, so too will your faithfulness. Timothy, the man of the Word, was able to set the believers an example in his faith and faithfulness. So, too, can you.

QUESTIONS TO CONSIDER

1. *You can't be faithful without faith and you can't have faith without the Bible. So, do you love the Bible? Are you filling your heart and mind with the Bible? Are*

you bolstering your faith with a growing knowledge of the character and works of God as he reveals himself through the Bible?

2. There is a temptation to believe that faithfulness is best proven in ways that are grand and public. Yet the Bible commends faithfulness in the little things and then invites opportunity to be faithful in bigger things (Luke 16:10). F.B. Meyer offers this challenge: "Don't waste your time waiting and longing for large opportunities which may never come. But faithfully handle the little things that are always claiming your attention." What are some "little things" in which you can prove your faithfulness today or this week?

3. In what ways do you think you are setting a good example to the people of your church in your faith and faithfulness? Pray and thank God for each of them. In what ways do you think you are not setting a good example to the people of your church in your faith and faithfulness? Pray and ask God for his grace to change you.

CHAPTER 6

Set an Example *in Your Purity*

There is a lot to love about the Bible. I could go on for hours about just how amazing, just how unique it is. The Bible offers us something so different from what we get anywhere else, something so opposed to our all-too-human expectations. When we live by the Bible, we live lives that are completely, radically counter-cultural.

We are drawing to the end of our look at 1 Timothy 4:12. All along I've been challenging you to see a glimpse of yourself in Timothy, in the young man the Apostle Paul mentored into ministry. Specifically, we've been considering Paul's challenge to his young friend: "Let no one despise you for your youth, but set the believers an example in speech, in conduct, in love, in faith, in purity." We've looked at speech and conduct, we've looked at love and faith, and we are left now with the simple word *purity*. Timothy is to be exemplary in his purity.

LOW EXPECTATIONS

We have discussed already that one of the challenges of being a young Christian is determining that you will not succumb to the low expectations of those who are older than you. And if there is any area of life in which older Christians have low expectations of younger ones, it is in this area of purity. Let's be honest: this is not entirely undeserved. It's not for nothing that Proverbs, a book written with young people in mind, says so much about the consequences of sexual sin and the joys of sexual purity. It's not for nothing that just a few verses later Paul will insist that Timothy treat "older women as mothers, younger women as sisters, in all purity" (1 Timothy 5:1) and that when he writes to Titus he insists that young women need to be self-controlled and pure (Titus 2:5). It should come as no great surprise, then, that old Paul tells young Timothy, "Set an example in your purity."

What does the culture around us expect of young people —people in their teens and twenties? It expects that you will use these years for exploration, for experimentation, even for exploitation. It expects that you will live these years wild and free, that you will sow your wild oats. A million sitcoms and movies and pop songs insist that these are the best years of your life and that you will be missing out, you will be less than a whole person, if you suppress or repress those desires. You've only got a few years before you'll be bound by responsibilities, so in the meantime run wild! Be free! Set an example in pursuing hedonistic pleasure.

HIGH EXPECTATIONS

In the face of such low expectations, the Bible comes through with the very highest expectations. Paul looks to young Timothy and charges him to be exemplary in his attitude, his imagination, his actions. When older people in his church ask "What does it mean to live a life of purity?" they should be able to point to young Timothy to find their example. Now that's a high challenge, but exactly the kind of challenge that is worthy of the Bible. The Bible never allows youth to be an excuse for sexual impurity or for any other lack of holiness.

Do you see how counter-cultural God's Word is? Where but the Bible would we find something as unexpected as this? Young Christian, you—you, of all people!—are to be the very model of sexual purity. God expects that older people who are struggling with sexual purity will be able to look to you and say, "I want to be like him" or "I want to be like her." Younger Christians who are struggling with sin should be able to look to you to find their example. They should all agree: he, she, sets an example.

INNER PURITY, OUTER PURITY

But how? How do you set this kind of an example? And what does this exemplary life involve? When Paul charges Timothy to be pure, he is undoubtedly thinking of the shame and disgrace that would come upon Timothy and his entire church if he was found to be committing sexual sin. Yet we know from reading the Bible that Paul would not only want Timothy to refrain from actually committing sin. He would first want him to emphasize an inner purity. After all, what's on the outside is always a reflection of what's on the inside. He would want Timothy to have pure hands, for sure, but also a pure heart, and a pure mind.

Pure hands. "Hands" symbolizes the entire body, of course. Your actions are to be marked by purity. You are not to commit sexual sin, but in God's world *not* sinning is not enough. No, you are to take actions that are consistent with a pure and holy life. You need to live in such a way that you are not expressing lust toward others but expressing love toward them instead. This is putting sin to death and coming alive to righteousness.

Pure heart. Of course the actions you take will be a reflection of what is happening within your heart. When the Bible speaks of the heart it refers to the desires, to the inner part of you that longs for fulfillment. Your longings eventually manifest themselves in your life, so you need to ensure that you are longing for what is right and good, what is pure and holy.

Pure mind. To have a pure heart and pure hands you must first have a pure mind. You need to be careful what you allow into your mind—what you see, what you read, what you hear. As Paul wrote elsewhere, "whatever is true, whatever is honorable, whatever is just, whatever is pure, whatever is lovely, whatever is commendable, if there is any excellence, if there is anything worthy of praise, think about these things" (Philippians 4:8). You must not allow yourself to live in a world of fantasy, a world in which you picture and ponder what God forbids.

Purity consists of pure actions, of course, but also pure desires and pure thoughts. Charles Simeon says it well: "Every word and every look, yea, and every thought, ought to be well-guarded, in order that Satan may not take advantage of us, and that not even the breath of scandal may be raised against us."[7] There's God's standard: not even the smallest breath of scandal. But always remember that what God desires, God provides. If God desires your purity, he gives you what you need to be pure and to love to be pure. He gives it in the Holy Spirit who dwells within you, the Holy Spirit who right now is calling you away from a life of sin and toward a life of purity.

Young Christian, God gives to you an important task: "Set the believers an example in speech, in conduct, in love, in faith, in purity." He would not demand what you could not do. At least, he would not demand what you could not do when you are indwelled by the Holy Spirit of God, the Holy Spirit who is far more committed to your holiness than you are to your sin. It is his joy to make you holy. It is his delight to help you become an example in your purity and, of course, in your speech, conduct, love, and faith.

QUESTIONS TO CONSIDER

1. *What is your greatest struggle when it comes to purity? What actions are you taking to combat this sin and to come alive to righteousness? Who have you enlisted to help you in this fight through conversation and prayer?*

2. *Do you really believe that you—even you—can be an example of purity? Do you really believe that your example can make a difference to others?*

3. *In what ways do you think you are setting a good example to the people of your church in your purity? Pray and thank God for each of them. In what ways do you think you are not setting a good example to the people of your church in your purity? Pray and ask God for his grace to change you.*

The Final Word

As we come to the end of this booklet, I want to return to a verse we encountered at the very beginning. Paul told young Timothy, "Train yourself for godliness; for while bodily training is of some value, godliness is of value in every way, as it holds promise for the present life and also for the life to come" (1 Timothy 4:7b–8). This is your challenge, too. Right now, in these years, at this stage of life, train yourself for godliness. There are many things that will and must capture your attention. There are many priorities competing for your time. None of them are more important than this: train yourself to be godly. And as you learn to be godly, be confident displaying that godliness so you, like Timothy, can set an example in all you do, in all you say, in all you model before a watching church. Set the believers an example of godliness!

NOTES

1   George Knight, *The Pastoral Epistles: New International Greek Testament Commentary.*

2   Philip Ryken, *1 Timothy: Reformed Expository Commentary.*

3   Bryan Chapell, *1–2 Timothy and Titus: Preaching the Word Commentary.*

4   John Stott, *The Message of 1 Timothy & Titus: The Bible Speaks Today.*

5   Charles Spurgeon, *All of Grace.*

6   Jerry Bridges, *The Practice of Godliness.*

7   Charles Simeon, *Horae Homileticae.*

THE
COMMANDMENT
WE
FORGOT

TIM CHALLIES

THE
CHARACTER
OF THE
CHRISTIAN

TIM CHALLIES

DO MORE BETTER

A PRACTICAL
GUIDE TO
PRODUCTIVITY

TIM CHALLIES

Do More Better

A Practical Guide to Productivity

by Tim Challies

**Don't try to do it all.
Do more good. Better.**

**Whether a student or a profes-
sional, a work-from-home dad or a
stay-at-home mom, this book will
help you structure your life to do
the most good to the glory of God.**

*114 pages
bit.ly/domorebetter*

Shortly after its release, *Do More Better* had received 173 reviews
on Amazon, with an average rating of 4.8 out of 5 stars. The book
sold more than 10,000 copies in its first two months. Here are Tim's
thoughts about this book:

*I am no productivity guru. I am a writer, a church leader, a husband, and
a father—a Christian with a lot of responsibilities and with new tasks
coming at me all the time. I wrote this short, fast-paced, practical guide
to productivity to share what I have learned about getting things done in
today's digital world. It will help you learn to structure your life to do the
most good to the glory of God.*

In Do More Better, you will learn:
* *Common obstacles to productivity*
* *The great purpose behind productivity*
* *3 essential tools for getting things done*
* *The power of daily and weekly routines*
* *And much more, including bonus material on taming your email
  and embracing the inevitable messiness of productivity.*

*It really is possible to live a calm and orderly life, sure of your responsibili-
ties and confident in your progress. You can do more better. And I would
love to help you get there.* — Tim Challies

Sexual Detox
A Guide for Guys Who Are Sick of Porn

by Tim Challies

"In an age when sex is worshiped as a god, a little book like this can go a long way to helping men overcome sexual addiction."
–Pastor Mark Driscoll, Mars Hill Church

"Online pornography is not just a problem for Christian men; it is THE problem. Many men, young and old, in our churches need *Sexual Detox*. Challies offers practical, doable and, above all, gospel-centered hope for men. I want every man I serve and all the guys on our staff to read this book."
Tedd Tripp, pastor, and author of Shepherding a Child's Heart

"Tim Challies strikes just the right balance in this necessary work. His assessment of the sexual epidemic in our culture is sober but not without hope. His advice is practical but avoids a checklist mentality. His discussion of sexual sin is frank without being inappropriate. This book will be a valuable resource."
Kevin DeYoung, pastor and author

"Thank God for using Tim to articulate simply and unashamedly the truth about sex amidst a culture of permissiveness."
Ben Zobrist, Tampa Bay Rays

"*Sexual Detox* is just what we need. It is clear, honest, and biblical, written with a tone that is knowing but kind, exhortative but gracious, realistic but determined. We have been given by Tim Challies a terrific resource for fighting sin and exalting Christ."
Owen Strachan, Boyce College

Can I Smoke Pot?
Marijuana in Light of Scripture

by Tom Breeden and
Mark L. Ward, Jr.

God made pot. It's natural. And it's legal in more and more places. And Christians are allowed to drink alcohol, right?

So really...what's the issue?

101 pages   bit.ly/POTBOOK

"Breeden and Ward offer a biblical, witty, and persuasive reply to a pressing question. *Can I Smoke Pot?* is a must read for young people and their pastors. I've already started reading selections to my own teens."
Chad Van Dixhoorn, Chancellor's Professor of Historical Theology, Reformed Theological Seminary – Washington DC

"This book deals with the important questions, using Scripture as its basis for ethical decision-making. With a good summary of biblical teaching on a number of relevant principles, it shows the possibility of medicinal use but rejects recreational use of marijuana. It is clear and engaging; it has sound arguments and sensitivity to our human condition."
Vern Poythress, Professor of New Testament Interpretation, Westminster Theological Seminary

"*Can I Smoke Pot?* is a good summary of the biblical teaching relevant to the use of marijuana. Authors Ward and Breeden have written it in language easily understood by young people. It makes a strong case against the recreational use of pot while recognizing the possible medical benefits of it.
Dr. John Frame, Professor of Systematic Theology & Philosophy, Reformed Theological Seminary

Licensed to Kill
A Field Manual for Mortifying Sin

by Brian G. Hedges

Your soul is a war zone.

Know your enemy.

Learn to fight.

101 pages
bit.ly/L2Kill

"Are there things you hate that you end up doing anyway? Have you tried to stop sinning in certain areas of your life, only to face defeat over and over again? If you're ready to get serious about sin patterns in your life—ready to put sin to death instead of trying to manage it—this book outlines the only strategy that works. This is a book I will return to and regularly recommend to others."

Bob Lepine, Co-Host, FamilyLife Today

"Rather than aiming at simple moral reformation, *Licensed to Kill* aims at our spiritual transformation. Like any good field manual, this one focuses on the most critical information regarding our enemy, and gives practical instruction concerning the stalking and killing of sin. This is a theologically solid and helpfully illustrated book that holds out the gospel confidence of sin's ultimate demise."

Joe Thorn, pastor and author, Note to Self: The Discipline of Preaching to Yourself

"Read this 'field-manual' and you will discover that you have a monstrous and aggressive antagonist who is aiming to annihilate you. It's your duty to fight back! Brian has given us a faithful, smart, Word-centered guide to help us identify and form a battle plan for mortally wounding the enemy of indwelling sin."

Wes Ward, Revive Our Hearts

Hit List
Taking Aim at the Seven Deadly Sins

by Brian G. Hedges

Pride, envy, wrath, sloth, greed, gluttony, lust: Not just corrupting vices, but gateway sins leading to countless others. Learn how to take aim at each one. Reach for holiness.

112 pp.
Learn more at bit.ly/HITLIST-7

"*Hit List* is a great book! Hedges brings the historic framework of the seven deadly sins into the 21st century. Brian's reading and research into historic Christian theology enriches this readable and thoroughly biblical examination and treatment of 'the big seven.'"
Tedd Tripp, author, conference speaker

"Satan destroys by cloaking his schemes in darkness. *Hit List* is a blazing floodlight—both convicting and gleaming with gospel clarity. For the Christian soldier eager to win the daily war against sin, *Hit List* is a welcome field manual."
Alex Crain, Editor, Christianity.com

"If you've ever heard you shouldn't envy (or get angry or lust or ...), but you don't know exactly what those sins look like in your everyday life—let alone the cure—then *Hit List* is for you. Brian has done his research, and I'm personally grateful for his insights on what's at the root of specific sins I deal with...and how I can break free. Read, repent, and live free!"
Paula Hendricks, Editorial Manager, Revive Our Hearts

"With characteristic depth, Brian unpacks an ancient formulation of our soul-sickness, while giving us the antidote of grace and gospel."
Del Fehsenfeld III, Senior Editor, Revive magazine

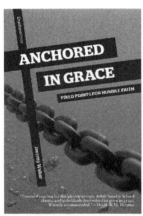

Anchored in Grace
Fixed Truths for Humble Faith

by Jeremy Walker

Clear truths from Scripture...

Central. Humbling. Saving. Comforting. God-glorifying.

Get Anchored.

86 pages
bit.ly/ANCHRD

"Rarely does the title of a book so clearly represent its contents as does this one. With brevity and precision, Jeremy Walker sets forth God's work of salvation in the believer from beginning to end. In a day when there is so much confusion regarding even the most fundamental truths of redemption, this concise yet comprehensive work is a clear beacon of light to guide the seeker and to instruct and comfort the believer."

Paul David Washer, Director, HeartCry Missionary Society

"As a pastor, I am always looking for a book that is brief, simple, and biblical in its presentation of the God-exalting doctrines of grace to put into the hands of believers. I think my search is now over!"

Conrad Mbewe, African Christian University, Lusaka, Zambia

"Crisp, clear, concise, and biblical, Walker's book offers up the doctrines of God's grace in a manner persuasive to the mind and powerful to the heart."

Dr. Joel R. Beeke, Pres., Puritan Reformed Theological Seminary

"A sure-footed journey...a trusted guide. Reading this book will both thrill and convict, challenge and confirm. Essential reading for discipleship groups, Adult Sunday School classes, and individuals determined to grow in grace. Warmly recommended."

Derek W. H. Thomas, Professor, Reformed Theological Seminary

Servanthood as Worship
The Privilege of Life in a Local Church

by Nate Palmer

We [serve] because he first [served] us. - 1 John 1:19 [sort of]

What ever happened to servanthood? Here is a biblical presentation of our calling to serve in the church, motivated by the grace that is ours in the gospel.

"In an age where the church can be likened to Cinderella—beautiful, but largely ignored and forgotten—Nate Palmer's brief book forces us to rethink both the church and our relationship to her. In an age where egocentrism ensures we sing, 'O say, can you see—what's in it for me?' on a weekly basis, Palmer forces us to say instead, 'How can I best serve the church?' Looking at the needs of others rather than one's own is possibly the most serious deficiency in the church today. Reading this book will help redress the deficiency. I heartily recommend it."
Derek W.H. Thomas, Professor of Theology, Reformed Theological Seminary (Jackson)

"Think of these pages as a handbook. It contains a sustainable, practical vision for serving in the local church that is powered by grace. Along the way, you'll get a mini theological education."
Justin Buzzard, pastor, San Francisco Bay Area, Buzzard Blog

"In our media-crazed, me-first culture, the art of the basin and the towel has been shoved off onto those who get paid to serve—certainly a call to serve in humility can't be God's will for all of us, or could it? Nate Palmer gets at the heart of our resistance.. I strongly recommend this book."
Elyse Fitzpatrick, author of Because He Loves Me

Who Am I?
Identity in Christ

by Jerry Bridges

Jerry Bridges unpacks Scripture to give the Christian eight clear, simple, interlocking answers to one of the most essential questions of life.

91 pages
bit.ly/WHOAMI

" Jerry Bridges' gift for simple but deep spiritual communication is fully displayed in this warm-hearted, biblical spelling out of the Christian's true identity in Christ."

> **J. I. Packer, *Theological Editor*, ESV Study Bible; *author*, Knowing God, A Quest for Godliness, Concise Theology**

"I know of no one better prepared than Jerry Bridges to write *Who Am I?* He is a man who knows who he is in Christ and he helps us to see succinctly and clearly who we are to be. Thank you for another gift to the Church of your wisdom and insight in this book."

> **R.C. Sproul, *founder, chairman, president, Ligonier Ministries; executive editor*, Tabletalk *magazine; general editor*, The Reformation Study Bible**

"*Who Am I?* answers one of the most pressing questions of our time in clear gospel categories straight from the Bible. This little book is a great resource to ground new believers and remind all of us of what God has made us through faith in Jesus. Thank the Lord for Jerry Bridges, who continues to provide the warm, clear, and biblically balanced teaching that has made him so beloved to this generation of Christians."

> **Richard D. Phillips, *Senior Minister, Second Presbyterian Church, Greenville, SC***